Learning to read. Reading to learn!

LEVEL ONE Sounding It Out Preschool-Kindergarten
For kids who know their alphabet and are starting to sound out words.

learning sight words • beginning reading • sounding out words

LEVEL TWO Reading with Help Preschool-Grade 1
For kids who know sight words and are learning to sound out new words.

expanding vocabulary • building confidence • sounding out bigger words

LEVEL THREE Independent Reading Grades 1-3
For kids who are beginning to read on their own.

introducing paragraphs • challenging vocabulary • reading for comprehension

LEVEL FOUR Chapters Grades 2-4
For confident readers who enjoy a mixture of images and story.

reading for learning • more complex content • feeding curiosity

Ripley Readers Designed to help kids build their reading skills and confidence at any level, this program offers a variety of fun, entertaining, and unbelievable topics to interest even the most reluctant readers. With stories and information that will spark their curiosity, each book will motivate them to start and keep reading.

Vice President, Licensing & Publishing Amanda Joiner
Editorial Manager Carrie Bolin

Editor Jessica Firpi
Writer Korynn Wible-Freels
Designer Rose Audette
Reprographics Bob Prohaska

Published by Ripley Publishing 2020

10 9 8 7 6 5 4 3 2 1

Copyright © 2020 Ripley Publishing

ISBN: 978-1-60991-454-7

No part of this publication may be reproduced in whole or in part, stored in a retrieval system, or transmitted in any form by any means, electronic, mechanical, photocopying, recording, or otherwise, without written permission from the publisher.

For more information regarding permission, contact:
VP Licensing & Publishing
Ripley Entertainment Inc.
7576 Kingspointe Parkway, Suite 188
Orlando, Florida 32819

Email: publishing@ripleys.com
www.ripleys.com/books
Manufactured in China in January 2020.

First Printing

Library of Congress Control Number:
2019942274

PUBLISHER'S NOTE
While every effort has been made to verify the accuracy of the entries in this book, the Publisher cannot be held responsible for any errors contained in the work. They would be glad to receive any information from readers.

PHOTO CREDITS

Ripley Readers

Shipwrecks

All true and unbelievable!

RIPLEY
PUBLISHING

a Jim Pattison Company

Table of Contents

Chapter 1
Exploring Shipwrecks

People have been sailing the seas for thousands of years. Not every ship returned to land. Let's explore some of the world's amazing shipwrecks!

How does a large ship end up at the bottom of the ocean? Sometimes coral **reefs** are to blame. The sharp coral can cut a ship open.

Bad weather is another way ships might sink. Strong winds can destroy sails. Very big waves can **capsize** an entire ship!

Believe It or Not... There are at least three million shipwrecks on the ocean floor. Less than 1 percent have been discovered!

People say that the **Bermuda Triangle** makes ships disappear. There is no proof that anything is truly dangerous about this area. But it is fun to hear the old sailor tales!

NORTH
ATLANTIC OCEAN

EU[

NORTH
AMERICA

AFRICA

Bermuda

Florida   Bermuda
           triangle

Puerto Rico

Reefs and storms have caused ships to sink. But they are not the only causes. Sometimes other ships or even airplanes sank ships.

The Japanese attacked Pearl Harbor, Hawaii, in December 1941. The U.S.S. *Arizona* battleship sank during the attack.

U.S.S. Arizona

U.S.S. _Indianapolis_

The U.S.S. _Indianapolis_ was attacked by a Japanese submarine in 1945. It sank in just 12 short minutes. The ship wasn't found for 72 years!

The RMS *Titanic* was said to be unsinkable. But the passenger ship collided with an iceberg on her very first sailing. The ship sank in 1912.

Believe It or Not... Ships are referred to as females. Sailors use terms like *she* and *her* when talking about a boat.

TITANIC
DISASTER
GREAT LOSS
OF LIFE
EVENING TELE
15TH APRIL 1912

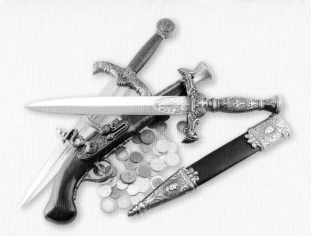

The *Mary Rose* first sailed in 1511. It fought many battles on the open seas. Underwater divers have found guns and swords from this wreck. They also found fiddles and dice!

Blackbeard is one of the most famous pirates in history! His ship was called the *Queen Anne's Revenge.* The ship sank off the Carolina coast in the early 1700s. It is now being carefully brought to the surface piece by piece.

Believe *It* or *Not*... The *Queen Anne's Revenge* originally belonged to the French. But Blackbeard and his pirate crew attacked the ship. The French surrendered it to the pirates.

The *Vasa* was a big embarrassment for the King of Sweden. The warship began its first voyage in 1628. It sank before it even left the harbor! The wooden ship is now on display in a museum.

Shipwrecks don't have to be hundreds of years old.

A ship named the *Panagiotis* ran aground in 1980. Researchers are still not sure what caused the shipwreck. Was the *Panagiotis* being chased by the Greek Navy? Was there a bad storm? Did the engine stop working?

A cruise ship called the *World Discoverer* hit an **uncharted** coral reef in 2000. The captain beached the ship. Everyone was safe. You can still see the abandoned ship in the Solomon Islands.

Water covers 71 percent of the entire world. It is no wonder there are so many shipwrecks that haven't been found!

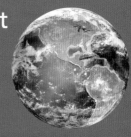

Here are some of the most famous that are still missing today:

SS BAYCHIMO

Nickname: "Ghost ship of the Arctic"

Date: 1900s

Ownership: Sweden, then Canada

Location of wreck: the Arctic

Cargo: furs for trading

Cause of wreck: a sudden storm that trapped the ship in ice

Believe It or Not... The *Baychimo* has been sighted more than a dozen times. The last sighting was in 1969. No one is sure if the ship finally sank into the ocean.

THE GRIFFON

Nickname: the "Holy Grail" of undiscovered Great Lakes shipwrecks

Date: 1679

Ownership: France

Location of wreck: The Great Lakes

Cargo: furs for trading

Cause of wreck: unknown

MERCHANT ROYAL

Nickname: "El Dorado of the seas"

Date: 1600s

Ownership: England

Location of wreck: near the Isles of Scilly

Cargo: Treasures, including 100,000 pounds of gold, 400 bars of silver, 500,000 **pieces of eight**

Chapter 2
Sunken Treasure

"Booty" is not just from pirate tales. Here are some sunken ships that were actually full of real treasure!

The sunken *San Jose* is thought to have more than $20 billion worth of treasure. There is gold and silver. There are also jewels! This treasure is known as "the world's richest shipwreck."

Mel Fisher found the sunken *Nuestra Señora de Atocha*. This Spanish ship sunk in 1622. It had more than $400 million in treasure!

The *São Vicente* was carrying treasure to France in 1357. It was attacked by two pirate ships! One ship was captured. Another got away with the riches.

Treasure doesn't have to be gold. A British ship called *Beatrice* was lost at sea in 1838. It was carrying a rare coffin. It belonged to an Egyptian pharaoh from 2500 B.C.!

Researchers find sunken treasure using the latest technology. They scan the ocean floors with underwater drones. Satellites can also find shipwrecks under the waves.

Chapter 3
Shipwrecks Not At Sea

We usually imagine shipwrecks in the ocean. But we can find them in other places, too!

A shipwreck in the desert? It's true! The *Eduard Bohlen* ran aground in 1909 in thick fog. Most shipwrecks are surrounded by water. But this ship is surrounded by sand.

The Great Lakes are called great for a reason. They stretch for hundreds of miles! The S.S. *Edmund Fitzgerald* was lost in Lake Superior in 1975. The waves reached 25 feet high in the storm. It is the largest ship to have sunk in the Great Lakes.

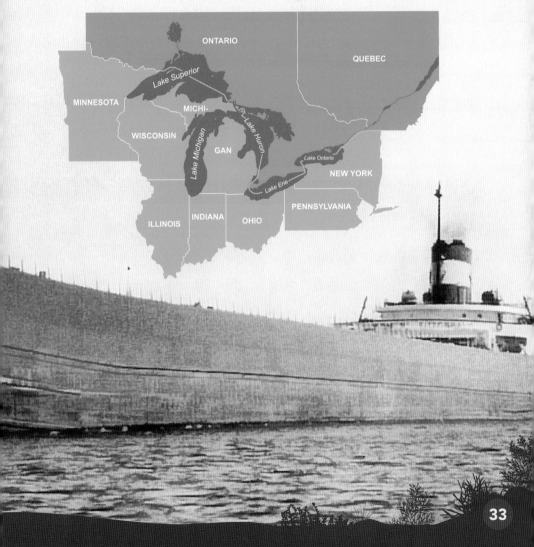

Great Lakes region

ONTARIO

QUEBEC

Lake Superior

MINNESOTA

MICHI-

WISCONSIN

Lake Michigan

Lake Huron

GAN

Lake Ontario

NEW YORK

ILLINOIS

INDIANA

OHIO

Lake Erie

PENNSYLVANIA

Chapter 4
Safety First

Shipwrecks are a scary thought. What do ships do to help keep their crew and passengers safe?

Today's ships have great communication technology. They also have **GPS** to guide rescue crews to their locations. Radar and satellites can warn captains about dangerous weather.

You will probably never find yourself on a sinking ship. But it's still good to be prepared! You may be on a little boat crossing a lake. You may be on a large ship sailing the seas. Safety should come first no matter what boat you are on.

- Always listen to the trained crew members

- Know where the life vests are located
- Know how to get to the lifeboats
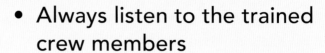
- Take swimming lessons

Chapter 5
Under the Water

A ship under water will change over time. The metal will rust. Animals will eat away the wood.

Shipwrecks in the Black Sea are special. There is no oxygen at the bottom of the ocean. The wrecks here don't **decay** like they do in other places!

Shipwrecks in Antarctica are special, too. **Bacteria** and wood-eating worms don't like the cold waters.

Leave the exploring to the experts when it comes to shipwrecks! Diving can be dangerous without training.

Hurricanes can be devastating. But they can also be helpful. High winds can uncover shipwrecks. Hurricane Michael in 2018 uncovered a shipwreck from 1899.

Sometimes people sink ships on purpose. These create **habitats** for underwater wildlife to live. They are also fun attractions for scuba divers!

The *Sea Tiger* was sunk in 1999 off Waikiki Beach. The ship rests between 80 to 110 feet down. It is popular with divers and submarine tours.

Believe It or Not... The largest **artificial** reef is an aircraft carrier! The Oriskany is a diving hot spot off the coast of Florida.

Shipwrecks can be lots of things. They can be habitats for animals. They can be peeks into the past. You never know which amazing piece of history will be discovered next!

The Greek ship SS *Stavronikita* sits perfectly upright. It is now home to many fish.

Glossary

artificial: Something man-made, unnatural.

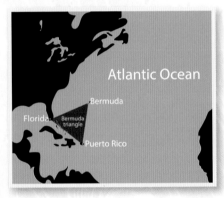

Atlantic Ocean
Bermuda
Florida
Bermuda triangle
Puerto Rico

Bermuda Triangle: an area in the North Atlantic Ocean where many airplanes and ships have disappeared.

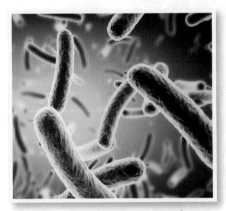

bacteria: microscopic single-celled organisms shaped like spheres, rods, or spirals. They live everywhere, including soil, water, and the bodies of animals.

capsize: to overturn.

decay: to rot, or undergo decomposition.

GPS: stands for Global Positioning System. A system that uses satellites to help navigate to a specific location.

habitat: the place or environment where a plant or animal naturally or normally lives and grows.

pieces of eight: Spanish currency based on the weight of silver. One silver piece of eight coin weighed about one ounce and had "8" stamped on it. Coins like these can be worth thousands of dollars today.

reef: an area with rocks, coral, or a ridge of sand at or near the surface of the water.

uncharted: not recorded on a map or plan.

 **RIPLEY® Readers**

All true and unbelievable!

Ready for More?

Ripley Readers feature unbelievable but true facts and stories!

 **Sharks!**
 **Trucks!**
 **Pets**
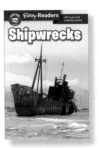 **Shipwrecks**

 **Weather**
 **Horses**
 **Bizarre Buildings**
 **Dinosaurs!**

**For more information about
Ripley's Believe It or Not!, go to www.ripleys.com**